HAL•LEONARD
INSTRUMENTAL
PLAY-ALONG

TENOR SAX

PEANUTS®

by Schulz

PEANUTS © United Feature Syndicate, Inc.

HOW TO USE THE CD ACCOMPANIMENT:

THE CD IS PLAYABLE ON ANY CD PLAYER, AND IS ALSO ENHANCED SO MAC AND PC USERS CAN ADJUST THE RECORDING TO ANY TEMPO WITHOUT CHANGING THE PITCH!

A MELODY CUE APPEARS ON THE RIGHT CHANNEL ONLY. IF YOUR CD PLAYER HAS A BALANCE ADJUSTMENT, YOU CAN ADJUST THE VOLUME OF THE MELODY BY TURNING DOWN THE RIGHT CHANNEL.

Visit Peanuts® on the internet at
www.snoopy.com

ISBN 978-1-4234-8689-3

HAL•LEONARD®
CORPORATION
7777 W. BLUEMOUND RD. P.O. BOX 13819 MILWAUKEE, WI 53213

Visit Hal Leonard Online at
www.halleonard.com

◆ BLUE CHARLIE BROWN

TENOR SAX

By VINCE GUARALDI

❷ CHARLIE BROWN THEME

TENOR SAX

By VINCE GUARALDI

◆ CHARLIE'S BLUES

TENOR SAX

By VINCE GUARALDI

◆ CHRISTMAS TIME IS HERE

TENOR SAX

Words by LEE MENDELSON
Music by VINCE GUARALDI

CHRISTMAS IS COMING

TENOR SAX

By VINCE GUARALDI

◆ THE GREAT PUMPKIN WALTZ

TENOR SAX

By VINCE GUARALDI

◆ 7 JOE COOL

TENOR SAX

By VINCE GUARALDI

◆8 LINUS AND LUCY

TENOR SAX

By VINCE GUARALDI

◆9 JUST LIKE ME

TENOR SAX

Lyrics by LEE MENDELSON
Music by DAVID BENOIT

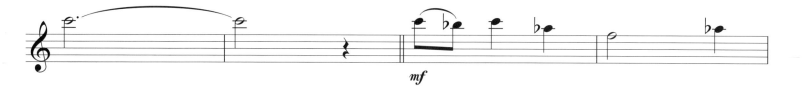

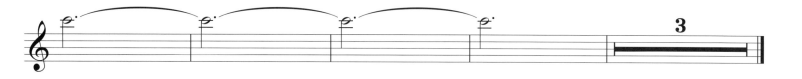

◆10 MY LITTLE DRUM

TENOR SAX

By VINCE GUARALDI

O TANNENBAUM

TENOR SAX

Traditional
Arranged by VINCE GUARALDI

OH, GOOD GRIEF

TENOR SAX

By VINCE GUARALDI

⒔ SKATING

By VINCE GUARALDI

TENOR SAX

◆14 RED BARON

TENOR SAX

By VINCE GUARALDI

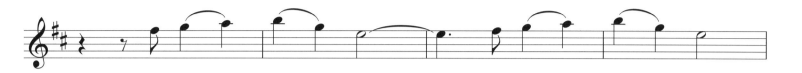

◆ WHAT CHILD IS THIS

TENOR SAX

Traditional
Arranged by VINCE GUARALDI